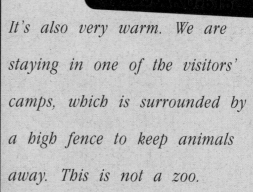

It's also very warm. We are staying in one of the visitors' camps, which is surrounded by a high fence to keep animals away. This is not a zoo.

It is a park for wild animals, spreading over 19,000 sq km (12,000 sq mi) of southern Africa. It is one of the largest wildlife parks in the world.

I have just finished getting my camera ready for an early start in the morning. Tomorrow we'll be going game-spotting for the first time. (Game-spotting is a term the local people use for watching the wild animals, or game, as they call them.) We all feel very excited.

We wake before dawn, have a quick breakfast, and load the car with our cameras, water, and food. As well as my camera, I need long telephoto lenses because we are not always able to get close to the animals.

HUNTING

WITH MY

Camera

At last we've arrived! After months of preparation our safari is about to begin. We have come to hunt — not with guns but with cameras!

After a long drive through farmland which no longer supports wildlife, we arrived at the park in time to see a beautiful sunset. As I write I can hear insects, bats, and other nighttime noises. It's so different from home!

Game-spotting starts early, while the air is still cool. This is not only for our own comfort but because wild animals are most active during the mornings and evenings, retiring to the shade in the heat of the day.

The first animal we spot is a graceful impala antelope. There are many small herds of impala in this park. The males have beautiful curved horns. As this is the lambing season, we search for newborn impala lambs and find some later in the day.

Shortly after seeing our first impala, we spot some giraffes. These elegant animals move very slowly as they browse among the leaves of tall trees and bushes.

Giraffes like to hunt out their favorite food — acacia leaves. They feed by wrapping their tongues around the leaves before chewing them off. Giraffes can go without water for days, relying on the moisture from vegetation, but they will drink regularly if water is available.

They prefer to feed in open parkland rather than in dense forest, so they can see their enemies approaching. Bull (male) giraffes grow to a height of about 5m (15 ft) while the cows (females) are a little shorter. Both can run at speeds of 50 kph (30 mph).

Later in the morning we hear some barking and expect to find dogs. Instead, we encounter a troop of baboons searching for food! Baboons travel in families, with the large males carefully keeping watch for predators. The females and their young travel through the long grass searching for seeds, insects, green shoots, and lizards to eat. If the males sense danger they bark loudly. Softer calls are used for keeping in touch with each other.

We return to camp for lunch and, like the animals, rest

during the heat of the day. When it gets cooler we resume game-spotting and continue until dark.

In Kruger we are not allowed to leave our cars unless we are in a fenced area. This is not just for our protection, but also to prevent the animals from being disturbed.

9

I have just finished cleaning my camera gear. Although it is the rainy season here, it is still very dusty, and I need to keep my camera as clean as possible. The film also needs special care to prevent damage by the midday heat. The temperature reached 44°C (111°F) today! I'm not used to such heat and find it very difficult to work.

Today is a day of contrasts. I photograph the largest animal in the park, and some of the smallest. The largest is, of course, the elephant. What fantastic animals!

In mid-morning a lone bull elephant visits the water hole. On its arrival, all other game leaves the water immediately, and an eland antelope seems very frightened. The elephant drinks deeply, then sprays water over itself before finishing up with a sand bath. Although the elephant seems calm, we still photograph from a distance, as elephants can run as fast as 40 kph (25 mph)!

Hunting with a camera includes searching for fascinating small animals and plants, as well as big game. This afternoon I discovered some paper wasps, and near the edge of the camp I found termites cutting lengths of grass to drag into their underground nests.

I also saw several rock lizards sunning themselves. Their bodies are so flat that they can easily hide in the narrowest rock crevices for protection.

Because we cannot leave the safety of our cars very often, it is difficult to photograph plants. However, I did find lovely sickle bush flowers.

It was very hot last night, and I tried to sleep with a wet towel over my body to keep cool. After such a tiring night, I am glad to start a little later this morning!

As the first rays of sun reach our camp, we watch and photograph a troop of vervet monkeys that has come through the fence. They are great fun to watch. It is tempting to offer them food, but this is discouraged, as the animals quickly become a nuisance.

Just outside the camp, we approach a large herd of buffalo. These huge, impressive animals have massive horns. They often form herds of a hundred or more. Again I use my telephoto lenses rather than trying to photograph them at close range.

15

The land occupied by the park is called the lowveld. Trees and bushes are scattered across the flat ground, giving the impression of a park rather than a forest. This makes it easier to photograph animals such as the beautiful nyala antelope we find.

Only the male antelopes have horns. We watch two sparring. They are young males preparing for the next breeding season, when they'll compete for female antelope.

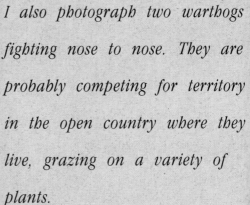

I also photograph two warthogs fighting nose to nose. They are probably competing for territory in the open country where they live, grazing on a variety of plants.

Warthogs are usually afraid of humans, but can become very dangerous when threatened or wounded. Their upper tusks rub against the lower tusks keeping the lower ones very sharp. However, these are not enough protection against the warthog's main enemies, which are lions, leopards, cheetahs, and wild dogs.

*I*t rained last night and cooled the air a little, so we all slept well. Another early start today. We visit a lake, where we spend most of the day. On the way there we spot impala, nyala, buffalo, warthogs, eagles, monkeys, and baboons. So far we haven't seen any lions or other large cats.

At the river we open the car windows and I prepare my camera. Soon, a bull kudu antelope approaches. It walks steadily, looking unhurried but alert. Its ears flick constantly as it moves its head from side to side. At the water's edge it pauses, looks around, and then drinks deeply before moving away to browse again.

The bulls have very long twisted horns. Their skins have a delicately marked pattern, which makes them very hard to see when they retreat into the bushes.

Various birds, including white-faced ducks, feed at the water's edge. Some, like the doves, arrive and leave in flocks. The white-faced ducks, however, spend most of the day on the lake feeding.

During the heat of the day we watch a male thick-billed weaver bird weave the beginnings of a nest from long threads of grass.

We are also lucky to see some crocodiles haul their bulky bodies out of the water to sun themselves.

In the evening a herd of hippopotamuses emerges from the water. They are difficult to photograph as it is getting dark, but this is when the hippos become active!

During the night they feed on vegetation, and at dawn they return to the water to rest and keep cool.

Unlike many other African animals, hippos must have a great deal of water. Although they have very thick hides, hippos still need to protect their skin from sunburn. They repeatedly sink below the

water's surface to cool off and moisten the skin. On very cloudy days, hippos will sometimes feed during the day.

Hippos are herbivores, so they don't eat fish while in the lake.

The animals graze by plucking grass and plants with their lips, then grinding them with their large molars.

The bulls have long canine teeth, which they use when fighting for cows or territory. They can inflict fatal wounds on each other when they fight.

Last night we lay in bed listening to the roars of lions and the howls of spotted hyenas. Again we leave camp before dawn, and as the sun rises we begin to search for the lion kill. It's not hard to find, as hyenas are waiting nearby for the lions to move away.

The lions killed a zebra during the night, and after eating well are lying down in the long grass to rest. Only the cubs seem to have much energy as they play with a length of the dead zebra's tail. I photograph the pride of lions for over an hour. The hyenas become impatient, but never once try to seize the zebra for themselves.

Sometime later we spot a vulture tearing at something on the ground. It can't have been a large animal, as there was only one bird. Vultures and hyenas play a very important role in the wild by scavenging the remains of dead animals, helping to keep the park clean.

As we travel slowly around the park we see many herds of zebra. They prefer the open grasslands and savannah to the more heavily shrubbed areas.

Zebras are sociable animals, moving around in family groups and associating with other animals, particularly wildebeest.

I never tire of photographing them as they graze, and find it remarkable that no two zebras have the same pattern of stripes.

Tomorrow is our last day in the park.

27

*F*or the last time I load my camera and film into the car. We have been really lucky seeing so many animals, but not all of them could be photographed successfully. Some were too far away even for my telephoto lenses, while others darted off as we approached. Some simply turned their backs on us, shunning our presence.

Many of the birds were hard to spot and approach. Birds have better eyesight than people, so they often saw us before we saw them.

African birds are usually very colorful. The glossy starling almost sparkles in the strong sunlight. The lilac-breasted roller looks even more colorful in real life than it does on film.

One bird is easy to spot — the world's largest bird, the ostrich. What it lacks in color it makes up for in character!

Heavy clouds accumulate all day, and as we leave the park we hear the sound of thunder rolling around the northern hills. Just at dusk the storm arrives. For two hours lightning flashes across the sky, accompanied by very heavy rain. It's a spectacular end to a thrilling week.

30

PHOTO INDEX